Bellerophon Coloring Book of New England Soldi⟨
The American Revolution
by Marko Zlatich
Illustrations by Donna Neary

The New England colonies (Massachusetts, Connecticut, Rhode Island, New Hampshire) and Vermont were the initial seat of the War for American Independence due in part to their martial spirit, which emerged early as a formidable force able to seriously challenge British authority in North America. By August 1775, General George Washington, the new commander of the colonial army surrounding Boston, could report that he had more than 22,000 New England soldiers in camp.[1] These troops were organized into provisional battalion-sized units and sent to Boston by their local vigilance committees to serve for the "duration of the present emergency." Benjamin Thompson, a "notorious Tory," caustically but accurately described the rebels in the following terms:

> The army in general is not very badly accoutred, but most wretchedly clothed, and as dirty a set of mortals as ever disgraced the name of a soldier. They have had no clothes of any sort provided for them by the Congress.[2]

These regiments represented their home colonies in the following proportions:

Colony	No. of Regiments
Massachusetts Bay	27
Connecticut	4
New Hampshire	3
Rhode Island	3
Total	37

Upon the British evacuation of Boston, the so-called "Cambridge" or "Grand American Army" ceased to exist. Its place was filled in January 1776 by the "Army of the Thirteen United Colonies." This army consisted of twenty-six foot regiments, one regiment of artillery, and one regiment of riflemen. The twenty-six foot regiments wore uniforms with buttons numbered to show the regimental rank in the line, and a set of regimental and grand division colors for each battalion was ordered. Though referred to as the Continental Regiments of Foot, all twenty-six regiments were raised in New England. Additional short-term service regiments and brigades were raised by the New England colonies from among the militia to do service in upper New York (especially around Fort Ticonderoga), in Canada, and elsewhere near the frontiers. On campaign, most of these troops wore their own clothing and carried their own equipment. A species of buff cap was referred to in many claims for losses incurred during these campaigns, indicating that a rough sort of uniformity was achieved if only in headgear. Some of the regiments intended to work on the Canadian frontier were specially equipped with snow shoes, ice grippers, large blankets, tomahawks, and other gear required for winter in the North.

Toward the end of 1776, Congress reorganized the Continental Army and authorized the New England states to recruit troops to form regiments in the following proportions:

Massachusetts	14
Connecticut	8
New Hampshire	3
Rhode Island	2

New England provided the recruiting ground as well for the Additional Continental Regiments of Foot of Henry Jackson, David Henly, William R. Lee (Massachusetts), Samuel B. Webb (Connecticut), Seth Warner (Vermont and New Hampshire), and Henry Sherburne (New Hampshire). Colonel John Crane's 3rd Continental Artillery Regiment was almost entirely formed in Boston, and the 2nd Continental Light Dragoons represented Connecticut in the Continental Corps of Light Horse. Moses Hazen's 2nd Canadian Regiment, Congress's Own, ironically was largely composed of New Englanders. And because of the advanced state of New England's economy, it was the principal site for the Continental Quartermaster General's department. The armory at Springfield, Massachusetts, which is still in federal service, was established in 1777. Clothing, ordnance, shoes, cartridge boxes, slings, and other instruments of war were manufactured both for the Continent and for individual states in especially established factories or under contract with local artisans.

From the beginning years of the Revolution, the New England troops were better uniformed and equipped than their comrades-in-arms from the other states. The textile industry of New England was the most advanced single industry in colonial America and thus could manufacture cloth and even ready-made clothing in quantities approaching sufficiency. And the open ports of New England served as depots for imported clothing, much of which was supplied to local forces. Between 1777 and 1780, the Boston firm of Otis and Andrews, acting as Continental clothing agents, supplied not only New England troops but also the New York and New Jersey lines and much of the Continental light horse and Continental artillery. There is ample evidence to suggest that clothing for New Englanders was in sufficient if not over-abundant supply. Although the basic blue-and-white color combination was in early evidence, it did not evolve into a universal New England pattern until 1779. In the interim, uniforms of brown, light blue, green, and even red could be noted. Even after the pattern was established by regulation, individual style interpretation was encouraged by General Washington.

In terms of human resources, New England was equally rich. Out of 20 "native" Americans to reach the exalted rank of Major General, 12 were New Englanders. To name a few we can mention Artemas Ward, first commander of the Continental Army; Nathanael Green, Washington's unofficial second-in-command; Richard Montgomery, the first officer of his rank to die in battle; and Israel Putnam, a hero of the French and Indian War.

In terms of active campaigning, the New England troops formed the first "Continental Army" around Boston and were the backbone of the Continental Army of 1776. During 1777 the New England regiments bore the main effort in the northern campaign to hold the Hudson Valley against Burgoyne's invasion from Canada. Practically the entire Massachusetts and New Hampshire lines were with Major General Horatio Gates's army at the decisive Battle of Saratoga, September 1777. Because of General Washington's high regard for them, the New England troops were not allowed to enjoy the fruits of this victory but were sent to Valley Forge to reinforce the main army. As a result, New England troops played a prominent part in the Battle of Monmouth, June 25, 1778. With no further threat to the Middle Colonies, most of the New England brigades ιeturned to their native states to reorganize. A portion, however, was dispatched under General John Sullivan to oust the British from Rhode Island. But for the 1779 expedition against the Iroquois (also under Sullivan), this was the last major campaign of the war for the New England troops. Until the end of the war, they served as a screen covering West Point, New Jersey, and New England itself from incursions by the enemy based in New York and Canada. Light infantry companies from each of the New England regiments were chosen to form the Light Infantry Corps under Major General Lafayette and thus were privileged to serve at Yorktown.

Like the rest of the Continental Army the New England Line suffered throughout the war from lack of manpower. As regiments gradually became weakened by desertions, casualties, sickness, and discharges, their total was reduced through consolidation. Between January 1777 and January 1781 there were fifteen Masachusetts Continental Line regiments arranged in numerical order according to the seniority of the commanding colonel. Henry Jackson's additional regiment entered the line in July 1780 as the sixteenth. But in February 1781, the Massachusetts Line was reduced to ten regiments. On November 4, 1782, the Line was again reduced, this time to eight regiments arranged as before in order of precedence according to the seniority of the commanding colonel. However, the ravages of expiring enlistments did not allow this arrangement to last: On June 13, 1783, at New Windsor Cantonment, the Massachusetts soldiers whose terms had not expired were merged into four new regiments under Colonels Michael Jackson, Henry Jackson, and Joseph Vose, and Lieutenant Colonel Commandant Ebenezer Sprout. In November 1783, these regiments were dissolved to form a new regiment, the Continental Regiment, under Colonel Henry Jackson.[4]

The Connecticut Line kept eight regiments in the field until July 1780 when a ninth regiment, formerly Colonel Samuel B. Webb's Additional Regiment of Foot, was added. Effective January 1, 1781, however, the number of regiments was reduced without affecting the actual number of men in the field. The old 3rd and 4th became the 1st Regiment under Colonel Durkee of the old 4th; the 5th and 7th became the 2nd under Colonel Swift of the old 7th; the 2nd and 9th became the 3rd under S. B. Webb; the old 6th Regiment became the 4th under Butler (formerly of the 2nd); and the 1st and 8th became the 5th under Sherman of the old 8th. Colonels Wyllys, Bradley, Starr, and Meigs were retired.[5] In January 1783, the 4th and 5th regiments were disbanded and their remaining enlisted men drafted into the 1st and 3rd Regiments and the 2nd Regiment, respectively.[6]

The 1st and 2nd New Hampshire Regiments served from November 1776 until March 1782, when they were reformed into the New Hampshire Regiment. The 3rd was discharged in January 1781.[7] The 1st and 2nd Rhode Island Regiments were completely discharged in May 1780 and a new regiment, the Rhode Island Regiment, was raised for service from June 1780 until the end of the war.[8]

The various state regular units only rarely continued beyond their statutory enlistment periods. However, they enjoyed the privileges accorded to regular troops and shared the rigors of campaigning when their local areas were threatened. Except for service in Canada and Northern New York, the state regulars raised in New England stayed there.

At the same time as the New England authorities were busy establishing their land forces, they were attempting to place their vulnerable coasts into some sort of defensive posture by launching their own navies and recruiting coast guard forces. Depending on the material and manpower resources available, the size of the navies varied from two galleys in Rhode Island to vessels of various tonnages in Massachusetts. Supplementing the regular navies were privateers operating on the basis of letters of marque issued by each state authority. Massachusetts and Connecticut each maintained a separate merchant navy to carry on trade with continental Europe. Throughout the war, the ports of Boston and Portsmouth, New Hampshire, served as the destinations of many valuable cargoes of arms, clothing, and other military equipage vitally necessary to all of the rebellious colonies.

With the fall of Philadelphia to the British in 1777, the Continental Navy became largely dependent on New England waters for homeports, recruiting bases, and construction facilities. Boston became the permanent site of the Continental Navy Board for the Eastern Department and as such played the most important role in the development and maintenance of the Navy during the Revolution. The significance of New England to the navy was such that "after 1776, all the new vessels added in America to the navy, with the exception of two or three, were either purchased or built in New England."[9] It was no accident that the first officer to receive the title of Commander of the Continental Navy was Commodore Esek Hopkins of Rhode Island.

Separate coast guard companies were raised at state expense for permanent garrisons at the more vulnerable ports. Their main duty was to man the guns of harbor fortifications, but they were often the first line of defense in case of enemy descent on the coast. Because much of its long coastline was a mere 20 miles north of British-held Long Island, the Connecticut shore was the venue of many pitched battles between local inhabitants and British and Loyalist attackers. In the opinion of a prominent historian, one of the great tragic episodes of the American Revolution was the attack on Fort Griswold, September 6, 1781, by turncoat Benedict Arnold, which culminated in the death of 75 men plus the garrison commander under circumstances highly questionable by eighteenth-century standards of warfare.[10] The Battle of Ridgefield and Danbury the year before had involved militia and Continental troops—ironically under Arnold— against 2,000 British soldiers led by Governor Tryon. Retaliatory raids on Long Island were made by state whaleboat services as well as by regular Continental units such as the 2nd Continental Light Dragoons under Major Benjamin Tallamadge. His raid on Fort St. George, Oyster Bay, in November 1780, which struck at Benjamin Thompson's forces, was such a well-engineered expedition it received mention in General Washington's dispatches in Congress.[11]

For the most part, the men of the coast guard served in their own clothing, although Connecticut deserter   descriptions indicate a certain degree of uniformity in brown straight-bodied coats, trousers, and round hats. Mitre caps also may have been worn in some companies (see *Caps and Helmets of the American Revolution*).

CAPTAIN, THIRD BRISTOL COUNTY (MASSACHUSETTS) MILITIA REGIMENT, 1774-75

When the political arguments precipitating the American Revolution boiled over into a test of strength, the Colony of Massachusetts Bay was fortunate that it could fall back upon one of the largest and most efficient militias in British North America. Dating back to the very founding of the Plymouth Colony, the militia was an integral part of colonial life. Moreover, most of the eligible males of the colony were free men and only a tiny minority belonged to any of the sects which abhorred the bearing of arms. Accordingly, the Provincial Congress of Massachusetts could call upon a substantial reservoir of manpower to take up arms and sustain resistance to the mother country.[1]

Organized into regiments assigned according to a quota of men aged from 16 to 60 in each county, the Massachusetts Militia was ready to support the new cause well in advance of actual hostilities. Records of townships and counties kept during 1774 contain numerous references to meetings of the militia to elect officers and to designate which members of the militia would serve in the minute companies. Among the records is that of the meeting of the Commission of Officers of the Third Regiment, Bristol County Militia, held in Norton on November 9. The commissioned officers attending the meeting voted to divide the regiment into two divisions, the East Division and the West Division. A total of 11 companies were identified and the field officers of the whole regiment elected.

At the same meeting the officers voted to adopt a uniform of blue coats faced red, blue breeches, white stockings, yellow buttons and a gold laced hat. Officers were to be armed with silver headed swords and spontoons (short pikes, spearlike weapons).[2] This uniform seems to have been adopted by other regiments. For example, a "Volunteer Company of Matrosses" (gunners), formed by the enrolled militia of the First Hampshire County Regiment outfitted itself in August 1776 in blue-faced red uniforms, white smallclothes, short black gaiters, and black fur caps with red cockades. Officers were distinguished by red plumes.[3] Although no description of the uniform of the Boston Regiment of Militia has come to light, contemporary press notices throughout the war mention its smart appearance and military bearing.

The typical equipment of officers and soldiers alike was "a good fire arm with a steel or iron ramrod, and a spring to retain the same, a worm, priming wire and brush, and a bayonet fitted to his gun, a scabbard and belt therefor, and a cutting sword, or a tomahawk or hatchet, a pouch containing a cartridge box that will hold fifteen rounds of cartridges at least, a hundred of buck shot, a jack knife and tow for wadding, six flints, one pound of powder, forty leaden balls fitted to his gun, a knapsack and blanket, a canteen or wooden bottle sufficient to hold one quart."[4]

[1] Charles Knowles Bolton, *The Private Soldier Under Washington* (New York, 1902), p. 8.
[2] Samuel Hopkins Emery, *History of Taunton, Massachusetts, from its Settlement to the Present Time* (Syracuse, N.Y., 1893), pp. 436, 473 n.2.
[3] Charles L. Merrick, ed., *History of Wilbraham U.S.A., Bicentennial Edition* (North Bennington, Vt., 1964), p. 215.
[4] *Continental Journal and Weekly Advertiser*, January 22, 1778.

COLOR GUIDE — Officer 3rd Bristol County Militia

Blue	Coat, slash on cuffs, lining, breeches
Red	Round cuffs, sash
White	Shirt, waistcoat, stockings; lettering on militiaman's cap, his belt
Yellow	Buttons
Gold	Hat lace, waistcoat lace
Silver	Sword hilt, spontoon point
Black	Scabbard, hat, shoes
Brown	Militia man's coat, spontoon staff
Grey	Militia man's cap

Captain, 3rd Bristol County (Massachusetts) Militia Regiment, 1774 - 1775.

PRIVATE, MASSACHUSETTS GRAND AMERICAN ARMY, JUNE-DECEMBER 1775

This soldier is typical of the civilian army that held its ground at Breed's and Bunker Hills on June 15, 1775, and forced the British to evacuate Boston for good in March 1776. Just one week after the battles of Lexington and Concord a "Grand American Army," as it was styled by the rebel press, was formed on paper. The Massachusetts Provincial Congress voted on April 23 to raise an army of 13,600 men and called upon the neighboring colonies to furnish enough troops to raise the total to 30,000. Within a month some 25,000 recruits were converging on Boston.[1] But, given the peculiar circumstances under which the Massachusetts Grand American Army was organized and maintained, there is strong evidence that the only regimental or military-style clothing worn at Bunker Hill was that which might have been personal property. It was not until 19 days after the battle that the Provincial Congress resolved:

> ... to provide 13,000 Coats, faced with the material of the coat, without lapels, short and with small folds. Each regiment to have its number on the pewter buttons.[2]

A Committee of Supplies was set up to apportion the manufacture of the coats among all the colony towns and districts. Along with each coat, the populace was requested to send two shirts, two pair of stockings and two pair of summer breeches.[3] On receipt of the "Provincial Cloathing," another committee was responsible for adding the numbered buttons to the coats, sorting them out in parcels suitable for a regiment, and shading them "as nearly as possible for uniforms."[4]

Our private could be Private John Bates of Captain John Ford's Company, Colonel Ebenezer Bridges's 27th Regiment. Private Bates died at Cambridge camp December 5, 1775, and his wearing apparel was sold at auction. The proceedings of the sale included a pair of stockings, a fine shirt, a piece of velvet cloth, a tow sheet, a pair of old breeches, a hat, a pair of old shoes, and an old coat and waistcoat, along with a "Coat Found by the Government" — one of the coats ordered by the Provincial Congress.[5] Among the many lists of clothing claimed lost by Bunker Hill participants, or claimed by next of kin, was one submitted by Silas Blood to the Massachusetts Council of State March 6, 1777, seeking compensation for the accoutrements taken from Abraham Blood of Groton, a 19-year old private of Captain Asa Lawrence's company in Colonel William Prescott's Regiment:

> The things lost as aforesd. are as follows (viz)

one Gun of the Value of	£3=0=0
a Powder horn 2/ bullet pouch 1/ knapsack 1/4	0=4=4
a Strait bodied all wool Coat 25/ a Jaicoat 13/4	1=18=4
a pair leather Breeches 18/ a woolen shirt 6/	1=4=0
2 pair of Stockings 7/ one pair Shoes 6/ Shoe bucks (?)	0=16=0
a blanket 12/ a hat 4/8	0=16=8
all which your Petitioner offers as part total	£ 7:19:4

> This may Certifey that Abraham Blood was a soldere in my Company & Slain in the Battle att Charlston and lost the above mentiond articals
>
> Groton March 13, 1777   Asa Lawrence Capt.[6]

In fact 108 coats were issued to Colonel Prescott's regiment on August 2, 1775.[7]

[1] Thomas J. Fleming, *Now We Are Enemies* (New York, 1960), p. 88.
[2] Peter Force, ed., *American Archives*, Series IV, Vol. 2:1486.
[3] Charles Knowles Bolton, *The Private Soldier Under Washington* (New York, 1902), pp. 124-25.
[4] "Resolve in regard to the furnishing of clothing for the Army, passed August 14, 1775," in XIX *Acts and resolves Public and Private of the Province of the Massachusetts Bay* (Boston, 1918).
[5] Wilson Waters, *History of Chelmsford, Massachusetts* (Lowell, 1912), p. 290.
[6] Petitions, etc. to the General Court of Massachusetts, Massachusetts Archives, Vol. 182, folio 228.
[7] Account Book of Supplies, Vol. 1, Ms. 92, Rare Books and Manuscripts Division, Boston Public Library.

COLOR GUIDE — Grand American Army 1775

Brown	Coat	Grey	Hat
Green	Blanket	Buff	Powderhorn, pouch and straps
Buff	Breeches	Red	Shirt
Light blue	Stockings	Black	Shoes
White	Buttons		

Private, Massachusetts Grand American Army, 1775.

THE SALEM RANGERS, 1775-76

The Salem Rangers of old Salem, Mass., were among the independent New England companies that rallied to the rebel cause early in the war. These companies not only provided men to the rebel cause, they served as training schools for future officers. Strongly emphasizing discipline, drill, and smartness of dress, they exposed the New Englander to an approximation of the military virtues necessary for an 18th-century officer. Among the senior Continental officers who received their initial training as members of independent companies we might mention Benedict Arnold (former captain and commandant of the 2nd Company of the Connecticut Governor's Foot Guards), Nathanael Greene (former private in the Rhode Island Kentish Guards), and Henry Knox (former lieutenant in the Boston Grenadiers). All rose to the high rank of Major General and held important commands.

In some instances the companies actually served on active duty alone, but for the most part, since they were part of the militia, the independents served alongside their less flamboyant comrades in arms. About the Salem Rangers little of record remains beyond a description of their uniform and a fragment on their active service. The Rangers were apparently at the camp in Cambridge — a diary entry of December 5, 1775, notes that prisoners taken by Massachusetts Bay privateers were marched through the camp to headquarters guarded by 16 "Rangers belonging to Salem, dressed in uniform."[1] On April 22, 1776, the company officers, Captain Joseph Sprague and Lieutenant Joseph Hiller, presented a petition to the town fathers requesting that the company of light infantry be made independent of the militia. At that time their uniforms were:

> a short green coat with gold trimming, cap of black beaver with four ostrich feathers and similar trimming; under dress white with black gaiters and ruffles over the hands.[2]

The chronicler of early Salem, Joseph B. Felt, concludes his mention of the Rangers with the information that because they were called upon to serve both by sea and on land they were disbanded. Our Ranger has daringly embellished his cap to suit his fancy.

Information on the uniforms of other independent companies may be of interest:

Connecticut

Governor's Foot Guards:

1st Company, Hartford: Red coats faced black, buff waistcoats and breeches, black fur grenadier caps.[3]

2nd Company, New Haven: Red coats faced buff, white waistcoats and breeches, silver buttons, ruffled shirts.[4]

Captain John Bigelow's Independent Company of Artillery: Short blue coats faced red.[5]

Rhode Island

Cadet Company of Providence: Scarlet coats faced yellow.[6]

Independent Troop of Horse of Captain-General's Cavaliers: Blue coats faced white, yellow buttons, white jackets, buff breeches.[7]

Massachusetts

Haverhill Artillery: Blue coats faced buff, buff waistcoats and breeches, yellow buttons, white stockings.[8]

Boston Independent Company (1777): Black coats faced red.[9]

Pittsfield Minute Company: Blue coats turned up with white.[10]

---

[1] *Extracts from the Diary of Lieut. Paul Lunt,* Proceedings of the Massachusetts Historical Society, 12.
[2] Joseph B. Felt, *Annals of Salem,* 2nd ed. (Salem, 1849), Vol. II:499.
[3] Henry Loomis Nelson, *Uniforms of the United States Army* (New York, 1959), p. 10; plate I.
[4] Edward E. Atwater, ed., *History of the City of New Haven* (New York, 1885), p. 649.
[5] *Connecticut Courant,* April 29, 1776.
[6] Winslow C. Watson, ed., *Men and Times of the Revolution, or Memoires of Elkanah Watson. . .* (New York, 1856), pp. 18-19.
[7] Item No. 15584, Miscellaneous Numbered Records of the Revolutionary War, Record Group 93, U.S. National Archives.
[8] George Wingate Chase, *The History of Haverhill, Massachusetts, to the Year 1860* (Haverhill, 1861).
[9] *Pennsylvania Gazette,* October 2, 1776.
[10] J.E.A. Smith, *The History of Pittsfield (Berkshire County), Massachusetts, from the Year 1734 to the Year 1800* (Boston, 1869), Vol. I: 205.

COLOR GUIDE — Salem Rangers, 1775-76

Green	Coat	White	Waistcoat, breeches, belts
Gold	Buttons, piping on coat	Brown	Musket
	Black	Cap, feathers, shoes, gaiters	

The Salem Rangers, 1775 - 1776.

THE REGIMENT OF ARTILLERY (KNOX'S) 1776 MATROSS

Within the new establishment of the Continental Army authorized by Congress for service during the year 1776 was a regiment of artillery to be commanded by Colonel Henry Knox of Boston. Consisting of a colonel, two lieutenant colonels, two majors and twelve companies of enlisted men and appropriate officers, the regiment initially mustered some 511 men on 6 January 1776. Its strength was almost entirely drawn from New England veterans of the seige of Boston.[1]

Following what must have been an extremely rapid training course, four of the companies under Major John Crane were dispatched in March to New York with 4 brass 6-pounders and 6 3-pounders. Three horses were required to pull the 6-pounder and two for the 3-pounder. A single company, that of Captain Popkin, remained in Boston.[2]

By April 29 the Continental Artillery in New York numbered eight companies established in an artillery park at Bayard's Hill near New York City. Captain Alexander Hamilton's company of New York Colony Artillery was to parade with the Continental Artillery and joined two companies already stationed at the Grand Battery (for the uniform of Captain Hamilton's company, see Bellerophon Books' *Paper Soldiers of the American Revolution*, $2.50 at your nearest bookseller). General Washington also ordered two companies to serve in Canada.[3]

The eight companies with Knox in New York took part in the entire New York Campaign which ended for them rather badly on September 15, when a goodly portion of the regiment were captured by the Hessians at Fort Washington. Colonel Knox narrowly escaped capture but did not succeed in bringing off his own clothing.[4]

The uniform we show here is that of a matross and is based upon regimental orders dated March 18, 1776 from Captain Stephen Badlam's company order book in the Boston Public Library.[5]

Summarizing the order and other information about the uniform found in other sources, we can describe it as follows:

Coat	Blue, red 2-inch wide lapels, cape, cuff, white lining, gold buttons
Waistcoat	White
Breeches	White, but actually received buff leather
Stockings	Blue
Half-gaiters	Black
Epaulettes	Two gold for field officers, one on right shoulder for captains and captain-lieutenants and one on the left shoulder for lieutenants.
Hat	Black with black cockade and gilt button

Special uniform buttons were to be provided, but probably did not reach the regiment before it was captured at Fort Washington.[6] Many of the survivors re-enlisted in Colonel Crane's regiment of Continental Artillery.

[1] Journals of the Continental Congress (Washington, D.C., 1905) Vol. VIII: 399; *American Archives*, Peter Force, ed., 4th series, Vol. I: pp. 633-64.

[2] Documents No. 18779, 18767 and 18785, miscellaneous numbered documents of the American Revolution, Record Group 93, National Archives.

[3] Writings of George Washington (Washington, D.C., 1934) Vol. IV: p. 460.

[4] Papers of Henry Knox, Massachusetts Historical Society, Vol. III No. 46.

[5] Manuscript no. MSC 35. 12, Division of Rare Books and Manuscripts, Boston Public Library; the Papers Henry Knox, roll III, item 59; items 93, 96 and 97; deserter descriptions *New York Gazette* and *The Weekly Mercury*, May 6 and June 10, 1776.

[6] Henry Knox Papers, ibid. III, item 31.

COLOR GUIDE — Colonel Henry Knox's Regiment of Artillery, 1776

Blue	Coat		Yellow	All buttons
Scarlet	Lapels, cuff, cape, heart on turnbacks		Brown	Canteen
Buff	Breeches			Musket
White	Waistcoat	Half gaiters	Black	Hat
	Coat lining	Gun sling		Shoes
	Stockings	Belts		Stock
			Grey	Haversack and strap

Matross, The Regiment of Artillery (Knox's), 1776.

22nd CONTINENTAL REGIMENT OF FOOT (RAISED IN CONNECTICUT) 1776

Roger Hooker was born in Farmington, Connecticut in 1731. A seafaring trader, he made 7 voyages to the West Indies before the War for American Independence. When the Lexington alarm in April of '75 reached Hooker's home town, he exchanged his account books for a musket, and joined a company of volunteer militiamen, all of whom were from Farmington. This first contingent of Connecticut troops to join the Army of Massachusetts [around Boston] probably had no uniforms as these men were individual volunteers who brought their own equipment, acoutrements and clothing into service.[1]

With the formation of the Army of The United Colonies in January 1776, Hooker was commissioned a Lieutenant in Colonel Samuel Wylly's 22nd Regiment of Foot, raised in Connecticut. This regiment served throughout the New York Campaign. Roger's seafaring background was utilized by General Washington, who placed Roger in charge of a flotilla or fireship which was expected to repel Lord Howe's attacking fleet.

Later, he served as a Brigade Major and as Commander of the 5th Company of the 22nd Foot. It was during the middle of the 1776 campaign that Roger, the prudent businessman, drew up a detailed list of his personal effects in case of loss of either the effects or of himself. This list survives and is quoted not only to help color Roger, but also to give you an idea of the things that an 18th century soldier needed to take with him for a year's campaign. This list is found in a photostat of Lt. Hooker's orderly book for July 19 to October, 1, 1776, in the Connecticut State Library.

"CampAtt N York May 13th 1776 An Inventory of what I now stand posset of Viz

1 Chest	2 Beaver hats 1 trm'd with gold
1 Box	4 White shirts
1 Scarlet Coat faced with buff with a gold Appolet	4 Check'd shirts
1 Blue Coat faced with Red	4 neck stocks
1 Lambskin Coat	3 silk handkerchiefs
1 Camblet Huzzar Cloak	1 Linnen handkerchief
1 Red Duffel Watchcoat	1 Haversack white goatskin
1 Red Baize Gown	1 bedrack
1 White Broadcloth Vest	1 Pillow & Pillowcase
1 White Coarse Vest	1 knapsack
1 Blue Coarse Vest	1 Napkin
1 Red Baize Vest	1 Bible
1 Lambskin Vest	1 Leather Pocket Book
1 White Cotton Ribb'd Vest	2 Orderly Books
1 pair Red plush Breeches	1 Cartouch box
1 pair white Ribb'd Cotton Vest	Bayonet Belt
1 pair Linnen Refferees	2 lancetts
1 pair Silver shoe buckles	1 Sugarbox
1 pair plated knee buckles	3 pewter plates
2 pair steel knee buckles	1 pewter Bason
1 silver mounted hanger	3 pewter spoons
1 pinchbeck watch	2 knives and forks
2 pair of Black silk knee garters	2 pewter Tumblers
10 pair of woolen stockings	1 penknife
4 pair Thread stockings	1 pair Leather Gloves
3 pair of shoes	1 pair Gaytors
	2 Blankets
	1 Silver Boosom, Brooch"

Although Hooker's inventory fails to include a firearm we have chosen to arm him with a fusil — a short, light musket commonly carried by 18th Century subaltern officers to go along with his "cartouch box."

Additional information on uniforms of this regiment is scarce and contradictory. All we can fall back upon are newspaper descriptions of deserters from the regiment. The first description appeared in the April 20, 1776 issue of the *Providence Gazette and Country Journal* and it said that Gideon Parker, about 5'4" tall with straight black hair, went away from Providence wearing a light colored uniform coat, a good pair of overalls and enough though somewhat dirty his other clothes not very good. Another regimental deserter is described in the *Connecticut Gazette* of April 19, 1776, who wore a red duffil greatcoat and below that a regimental coat with red facings.

22nd Continental Regiment of Foot (Raised in Connecticut) 1776.

This regiment served to the end of 1776 when its men were mustered out of service to return home to Connecticut; many individuals reenlisted in the Connecticut line, but as such, the 22nd regiment ceased to exist further.

[1] Edward Hooker, *The Descendants of Rev. Thomas Hooker of Hartford, Connecticut 1586-1908* (Rochester, 1909), p. 69.

COLOR GUIDE — Lt. Hooker 22nd Continental Regiment 1776

Scarlet	Coat
Buff	Lapels, cuffs, cape
Blue	Waistcoat
Red	Breeches
White	Shirt, stock ruffles, stockings, sword belt, cartridge belt, fusil sling
Gold	Epaulette, hat binding, looping and tassel; sword hilt, scabbard tip; buttons
Brown	Fusil
Black	Garters, hat, shoes

SEAMAN, GUARD SHIP *DEFENCE*, MASSACHUSETTS STATE NAVY, 1778

Second only to the Continental Navy in importance, the Massachusetts State Navy, augmented by privateers, was the largest single armed force maintained by the thirteen colonies. During the revolution, the state commissioned about 35 men-of-war, including two ranked as frigates. Surviving records list at least 300 Boston ships granted letters of marque — authorization to engage in privateering. Postulating an average of 100 men per vessel, one source estimates that Massachusetts sent as many as 60,000 men to sea between 1775 and 1783.[1] While this may be a high estimate, nonetheless the vast number of ships of all classes flying Massachusetts colors constituted a force of many more men than the combined rebel *armies* in the field.

During its existence, the State Navy served as a coast guard, high seas and home fleet, and merchant marine. Its actions ranged from cutting up enemy merchant convoys to broadside engagements, such as that between the *Tyrannicide* and the *Revenge*, a Jamaica privateer. However, the bulk of the fleet suffered a premature and inglorious end in July 1779 — most of the ships were scuttled off Penobscot when a Massachusetts-sponsored expedition against the British garrison there failed dismally.[2]

A proper uniform of green and white was prescribed for State Navy officers on April 29, 1776. Their flag was white with a green pine tree in the middle and an inscription, "APPEAL TO HEAVEN."[3] Uniform dress regulations for seamen and marines have yet to be found; however, the Massachusetts Archives contain many lists of "slops," or clothes for State Navy enlisted ranks. Typically, shirts, breeches, sailors' trowsers, checked or speckled shirts, hats, and jackets were issued in quantities sufficient for a whole ship's company. A suit of Continental and State ensigns and pendants was also made for each ship. The usual hand weapons were cutlasses, pistols, pikes, and muskets. The marines were charged with drums and fifes, but in other respects seem to have received the same clothing as the seamen.[4]

Another basis for the figure shown here is one of the few surviving descriptions of a Massachusetts State Navy seaman, that of Mathew Hays, who deserted July 6, 1778, from the Guard Ship *Defence*, Commanded by Captain Jeremiah Clark.[5]

[1] Justin Winsor, ed., *The American Revolution, A Narrative Critical and Bibliographic History* (New York, 1972), pp. 585-87.
[2] *ibid.*, p. 582.
[3] *Naval Documents of the American Revolution* (Washington, D.C., 1969), Vol. IV, p. 1303.
[4] Massachusetts Archives, Volumes 150, 151, 272, 313 *passim.*
[5] *Independent Ledger and American Advertiser*, July 20, 1778.

COLOR GUIDE — Massachusetts Guard Ship

Brown	Jacket
Red	Shirt
Grey	Trousers
Black	Hat, shoes, sword belt, scabbard, cutlass hilt, handkerchief around neck
Yellow	Hat plate

Seaman, Guard Ship Defence, *Massachusetts State Navy, 1778.*

CAPTAIN OF GRENADIERS, 26TH CONTINENTAL REGIMENT, MASSACHUSETTS, 1776

The 26th Continental Regiment was authorized by Congress in January 1776 and was raised from Massachusetts veterans of the siege of Boston. Its commander was Colonel Laomi Baldwin, an apple grower from Woburn, Mass., who had the distinction of having participated in the battle of Concord Bridge, April 19, 1775.

In May 1775, shortly after it was formed, the regiment marched to New York to serve in Colonel John Glover's brigade,[1] which was the rear guard covering the retreat of the American forces as General Howe drove them up Manhattan Island. In this key role, the regiment distinguished itself at Eastchester on October 18. As the revolutionary army retreated toward White Plains, Colonel Glover's brigade, four regiments totaling about 750 men, held its ground against an army of 4,000, and even forced the British advance guard to fall back on its main body.[2] At its last muster in December 1776, after Washington's army had crossed over into Pennsylvania, the regiment still had 443 men present and fit for duty, an admirable showing after heavy campaigning.[3] The unit left the service at the end of the year.

The figure shown here is unusual: a Colonial grenadier. This class of American infantryman is rarely encountered in the literature of the American Revolution. Grenadiers are more commonly associated with the standing armies of Europe, in which regiments were organized into line, light infantry, and grenadier segments. That the 26th Continental Regiment had a grenadier company is attested by the account book of Captain Thomas Mighill.[4] It specifically cites the purchase of "Grenadiers caps" for his company. The mitre cap illustrated may not be the type worn by this regiment, but is of Massachusetts origin and bears the GW cypher, standing for George Washington.

The uniform is based on an invoice of Colonel Baldwin's own clothing and camp equipage. Among other items inventoried are: a deep blue coat and a light blue homespun jacket, a London brown coat of uniform with silver epaulettes, a silver and ivory hilted hanger, silver shoebuckles, and a neat pair of gaiters. In addition Baldwin had a saddle and bridle, a pair of trooping pistols, and a silver gorget.[5] The style of uniform is derived from a recruiting poster published in Massachusetts in March 1777.

[1] Returns of the Army under General Washington, Jacket 12-2, item 33 *et seq.*, Revolutionary War Rolls, Record Group 93, Revolutionary War Records, National Archives, Microcopy 246, Reel 137.
[2] Bruce Bliven, Jr., *Battle for Manhattan* (Baltimore, 1956), p. 104.
[3] Returns of the Army . . . *op cit.*, Jacket 12-3, item 43.
[4] Account Book of Captain Thomas Mighill, Vol. 174, Miscellaneous numbered account books, Record Group 93, Revolutionary War Records, National Archives.
[5] "An Exact Invoice of Cloathing Camp Equipage belonging to Laomi Baldwin Colonel of the 26th Regt in the Continental Army Stationed at New York at New York June 10th 1776." Manuscript, David Library of the American Revolution, Washington Crossing, Pa.

COLOR GUIDE — 26th Regiment of Foot

London Brn	Coat, lapels, cuffs
Silver	Buttons, epaulettes, buckles
Light blue	Jacket
White	Breeches, lining of jacket, belts
Ivory	Hanger hilt
Black	Boots
	Scabbard
Brown	Fusil
Yellow	Powder horn

Captain of Grenadiers, 26th Continental Regiment, Massachusetts, 1776.

FIFER, 1st CONNECTICUT REGIMENT 1777-1778

On February 15th, 1777, the Connecticut Council of Safety voted that Colonel Jedediah Huntington's 1st Connecticut battalion would have clothing of the red coats brought in a prize vessel, which clothing was to be delivered to Norwich, Connecticut.

On March 8, the Council of Safety voted that the regiment also receive 700 hats. By May 21st, Colonel Huntington could report that most of his regiment was clothed, as requested by the Council of Safety.[1] On June 7, 1777, the first battalion received enough white cloth to make waistcoats and a sufficient supply of cartridge boxes. They also received 800 pair of stockings, 1,100 shirts, 800 pair of shoes, 500 waistcoats, 700 hats and 700 linen overalls.[2] By June 5, men who had received the new clothing felt tempted to desert and were advertised accordingly in the local newspapers. Noted in the *Connecticut Gazette and Universal Advertiser* of 25 July, 1777, was a David McDuel, who was about 5'5" high, 20 years old, who had on a red regimental coat. The issue of 19 September listed one John Wrighben, also 5'4" (sic) high, brown hair, blue eyes, a scar on a cheek, who had on a red regimental coat. He deserted. Our figures in this plate are based on a large group advertised by Lt. David Dorrance who deserted from the regiment on January 31, 1779. They were listed as Corporal Judah West, who had on a scarlet coat faced with white, a white jacket and breeches and a small round hat; Ephriam Cox, a fifer who was about 5'10" high, 20 years of age, light complexion and hair, had on a snuff colored coat, faced with light brown, white jacket and breeches, small round hat bound with white; Robert Herd, a private, 5'11" high, light hair, complexion and eyes, who had on a red coat faced with white, brown vest, black breeches edged with red, and a small round hat; and Joseph Billings, also 5'11", about 22 years old, light hair and complexion and dark eyes, who wore a red coat with blue facings, white jacket and breeches and a small round hat. Captain John Barnard's Company Clothing book for 1777, in the Connecticut Historical Society indicates each man had a striped vest.

Summarizing the information we have on the Connecticut Line for the period 1777 through 1778, we can say that the first regiment had scarlet coats, faced white, white vests, buff breeches and round hats. The second had dark brown coats faced white, with brown vests and breeches, flopped hats turned up on one side; and green faced brown coats for the drums and fifes. The third had light brown coats faced red with green vests and breeches. The fourth had dark brown coats faced red, with light brown smallclothes and yellow bound hats and the fifth had yellow faced brown for the drums and fifes. The sixth had blue coats faced white, with white smallclothes and leather caps. The seventh had light brown coats faced blue and the eighth had blue coats faced red. All in all, the Connecticut Line was a very proud organization, proud of its uniforms and of the fact that it was able to provide for its own men out of its own stores and supplies. The Connecticut regiments served together throughout the war and little can be said more about these troops except that they were a steadfast group of soldiers who did great honor to their home state.

[1] Charles J. Hoadly, *ed.*, *Public Records of the State of Connecticut* (Hartford, 1894) Vol. I.
[2] Jedediah Huntington to Andrew Huntington, 7 June 1777, Miscellaneous Numbered Documents, No. 34817, War Department Collection of Revolutionary War Documents, Record Group 93, National Archives.

COLOR GUIDE — 1st Connecticut Regiment 1777-1778

Red	Private's Coat
	Cord and tassels suspending fife case
	Edging on private's breeches
Light brown	Fifer's lapels, cuffs and cape
	Private's waistcoat
	Fife
Grey-brown (Snuff)	Fifer's coat
White	Fifer's waistcoat, breeches, hat binding
	Fifer's shoulder belt
	Buttons, Stocks, Shirts,
	Private's coat lining
	Private's slings and equipment
Grey	Stockings
	Half gaiters
Yellow	Fife case, Fife ferrels
Black	Hats, shoes, Private's breeches
Brown	Musket

Fifer, 1st Connecticut Regiment, 1777 - 1778.

LIEUTENANT COLONEL PAUL REVERE,
MASSACHUSETTS STATE TRAIN OF ARTILLERY, 1777-79

By resolution of the Council of State of Massachusetts adopted April 14, 1777, a regiment of artillery in the service of the colony was raised for a term of three years. Under the command of Colonel Thomas Crafts of Leominster, the regiment was to consist of ten companies of matrosses (gunners) together with a full staff of field officers. Normally on duty within Massachusetts, the regiment could leave the state with the concurrence of the General Court or Council of State.[1] Each volunteer matross was promised 48 shillings as wages per month, good quarters, and a suit of regimental clothes per year, as well as a blanket and arms and accoutrements.[2] The regiment's first assignment was to assemble on Boston's Congress Street and give thirteen discharges with brass cannons and powder manufactured in Massachusetts — a salute to the first anniversary of American independence. Colonel Crafts illuminated the Artillery Park on Boston Common with bursting shells and fireworks. The celebrants that day drank thirteen toasts, for each of the rebellious colonies, punctuated by the discharges of cannon.[3]

Questions have been raised about what happened to Paul Revere after his famous midnight ride (depicted in Bellerophon's *Coloring Book of the American Revolution)* into history. This is what happened: Paul Revere was appointed a major in the state artillery regiment on April 10, 1777. On August 27, 1777, Major Revere led a detachment of the regiment along with a large body of militia to Watertown, Mass., as an escort for enemy prisoners taken at the Battle of Bennington.[4] During the months of July and August, 1778, the regiment became part of a brigade under Colonel John Crane, Continental Artillery, to serve in Major General Sullivan's unsuccessful campaign to take Newport, R.I., from the British. The regiment returned to Boston, and Revere, now a lieutenant colonel, was placed in command of Fort William. This quiet garrison duty lasted for less than a year. In July 1779, he was placed in command of the Massachusetts artillery in the state's attempt to retake Penobscot from the British. This expedition was a total disaster and our hero ended up sharing in the disgrace. For the next two years, Revere was engaged in defending himself against charges of abandoning troops and supplies and disobeying orders. He was totally cleared of charges against him in 1783, but his military career had been ruined.[5] The regiment was discharged in 1780.

The blue-faced red uniform the colonel wears is based on deserter descriptions published in Boston newspapers between 1777 and 1779, records of the Massachusetts Board of War (which was responsible for providing the State Train of Artillery with clothing, equipment, and provisions), and a miniature portrait of Colonel Thomas Crafts. Enlisted matrosses wore similar uniforms but without the gold trim, with yellow instead of gold buttons. Drummers wore red uniforms. A new uniform of blue-faced blue was issued in 1779.[6]

[1] Massachusetts General Court Records, Massachusetts Archives, Vol. 37, Section 1, folio 187-90.
[2] *Boston Gazette*, May 26, 1777.
[3] *ibid.*, July 7, 1777.
[4] Charles Ferris Gettemy, *The True Story of Paul Revere* (Boston, 1905), pp. 150-51.
[5] *ibid.*, pp. 216-17.
[6] Massachusetts Board of War Minutes, Massachusetts Archives, Vol. 150, *passim.*; *Continental Journal and Weekly Advertiser*, February 19, 1778; *Boston Gazette*, November 10, 1777 and March 2, 1778; *Independent Chronicle*, March 4, 1779.

COLOR GUIDE — Paul Revere

Blue	Coat
Scarlet	Lapels, cuffs
White	Shirt, ruffles at neck and wrists, stock, lining of coat, stockings
Black	Hat, shoes
Gold	Edging on coat, lapels, pocket, waistcoat piping, buttons and buttonholes, hat button and looping, coat buttons, edging on cuffs, epaulettes
Crimson	Sash
Light blue	Gun carriage
Brass	Gun barrel

Lieutenant Colonel Paul Revere, Massachusetts State Train of Artillery, 1777 - 1779.

CAPTAIN, LIGHT INFANTRY COMPANY, SECOND MASSACHUSETTS CONTINENTAL INFANTRY REGIMENT, 1778-79

The hardships of Fort Ticonderoga and Valley Forge were experienced by the 2nd Massachusetts Continental Infantry. Under the command of Colonel John Baily, the regiment joined General St. Clair's northern army holding Fort Ticonderoga and was stationed at Mount Independence. After the fall of Ticonderoga on July 5, 1777, the 2nd Massachusetts participated in the long retreat St. Clair compelled his troops to endure, ending at Fort Stanwix on the eastern shore of the Hudson River. There they joined New York units holding the fort against a siege by Colonel Barry St. Leger's combined force of Indians, Tories, and British regulars. This siege has a special place in American history — the first time the Stars and Stripes is known to have been carried in battle. The flag included pieces of Captain Abraham Swartwout's blue cloak.[1] In 1778, the 2nd Massachusetts was stationed at Fishkill, N.Y.

The illustration portrays Captain Judah Alden, commander of the regiment's Light Infantry Company, as he might have appeared in 1778 or 1779. The end wings are from a pen-and-ink sketch of Captain Alden by Colonel Thadeus Kosciusko, made at Valley Forge. Over his shoulder is a greatcoat for which Captain Alden petitioned the Council of State of Massachusetts on January 21, 1779.[2] Records of the state Board of War show that Alden received four yards of grey cloth the next day.[3]

The regiment's first uniforms were issued by the Continental Store at Albany, N.Y., in December 1777. The exact style of uniform is unknown, but existing records state that substantial amounts of green and red cloth were made available, suggesting the uniform was green and red at that time;[4] later descriptions, however, indicate a blue-and-white uniform. (The only deserter descriptions that have come to light concern recruits who deserted before July 1777, when the regiment had not been uniformed.) Writing in December 1778 to the Massachusetts Board of War from Fishkill, Lieutenant Colonel Ezra Badlam said his soldiers were "in health and high Spirits and well Clothed."[5] The style of uniform here is drawn from a description by a German officer who saw a Captain Hayward bearing a flag of truce; Hayward is described as wearing a blue coat with white cuffs.[6] In a letter to the Board of War on October 5, 1779, appealing for officers' clothing, Colonel Badlam said in a footnote that "the Uniform of our Regiment is blue turned up with white."[7]

[1] Harlan Hoyt Horner, *The American Flag* (Albany, 1910), p. 21.
[2] Council Papers, 2nd Series, Massachusetts Archives, Vol. 175, p. 102.
[3] Board of War Papers, Massachusetts Archives, Vol. 151, p. 81.
[4] Revolutionary War Rolls, Massachusetts, Jacket 3-1, Item 17, "Colonel Bailey's acct. with the Public Store for Clothing at Albany, May 1777," Record Group 93, Microcopy 246, National Archives.
[5] Board of War Letters, Massachusetts Archives, Vol. 153, p. 132.
[6] *Writings of George Washington* (Washington, D.C., 1937), Vol. 16, p. 170n.
[7] Board of War Letters, Massachusetts Archives, Vol. 153, p. 310.

COLOR GUIDE — Lt. Judah Alden, 2nd Massachusetts

Blue	Coat, lapels, cape	
White	Cuffs, turn backs on coat, overalls	
	Horsehair on crest of cap, turban around cap	
	Shirt, ruffles at neck and cuffs	
Black	Cap	Shoulder belt
	Stock	
	Shoes	
	Garter	
Silver	Buttons	Shoulder wings
	Sword	Belt buckle
Grey	Greatcoat hanging over shoulders	
Scarlet	Waistcoat	

Captain, Light Company, 2nd Regiment (Massachusetts), 1779.

SERJEANT, COLONEL HENRY JACKSON'S ADDITIONAL CONTINENTAL REGIMENT OF FOOT, 1779-80

One of three Additional Regiments of Foot raised during 1777 in Massachusetts, Henry Jackson's command early established and later maintained a reputation as one of the elite units of the Continental Army. Following its organization as an independent unit, the regiment marched to join the main army in October 1777, and Major General William Heath noted in his diary that "the regiment, although small, made a good appearance."[1] There is good evidence that, at this stage, the men were clothed in red uniforms — we find Colonel Jackson's friend, General Henry Knox, repeatedly warning against that color.[2] The field officers were generously allowed to purchase confiscated gold lace for epaulettes, and to trim their waistcoats, from the Massachusetts Bay storehouse at discount prices.[3]

Indicating high regard for his regiment, General Washington selected Colonel Jackson to lead a detachment from his command as the vanguard entering Philadelphia after its evacuation by the British Army in June 1778. Jackson's orders were to safeguard lives and prevent plundering.[4] The tenure of the regiment at Philadelphia was relatively short, as it was ordered northward to join General John Sullivan in Rhode Island. Arriving in August, it participated in the battles and siege of Newport.

While the regiment was stationed at Providence, a General Order of October 18, 1778, was issued prescribing blue and buff as the uniform for the Additional Regiments commanded by Colonels Jackson, Smith, and Henley.[5] A more complete description of the uniform was drafted in July 1779:

> Blue [coats] faced with Buff and white under Clothes for the officers, White Vests blue Overalls for the non Commsd officers and Soldiers the lapels of the Coats to be made open Open Holes bound Hatts and Shoulder Knots for the Non-Commissiond officers & Music   Black Stocks.[6]

By August, 1779, the regimental surgeon, Dr. James Thatcher, would boast to his diary that "our regiment consists of about 400 men in complete uniform, well disciplined and not inferior to any in the Continental Army."[7]

On July 23, 1780, Jackson's Additional Regiment was redesignated the 16th Regiment of the Massachusetts Continental Line. Colonel Jackson remained with the Continental Army throughout its existence, and was retained by Congress as Colonel of the Continental or 1st American Regiment from November 3, 1783, until June 20, 1784, earning the distinction of being the last commander of a Continental infantry regiment.

An anonymous portrait of an unknown officer in the collection of the Essex Institute, Salem, Mass., was used as the model for this figure.

---

[1] William Abbatt, ed., *Memoirs of Major General William Heath* (New York, 1901), p. 119.
[2] Papers of Henry Knox, Microfilm, Roll IV:75.
[3] Board of War Orders, Massachusetts Archives, Vol. 270.
[4] Lieutenant Colonel Tench Tilghaman to Colonel Henry Jackson, Head Quarters, June 18, 1778, in J.C. Fitzpatrick, ed., *The Writings of George Washington* (Washington, D.C., 1934), Vol. 12:88.
[5] Headquarters Orderly Book (Volume 26, p. 39), War Department Collection of Revolutionary War Record Books, Record Group 93, U.S. National Archives.
[6] "Return of Cloathing necessary to be procured for the Officers & Men of Col Henry Jackson's Regiment for the ensuing Winter, Camp Providence, July 1779," MS Ch.M.3.6.139, Rare Books and Manuscripts Division, Boston Public Library.
[7] James Thacher, *Military Journal of the American Revolution* (Hartford, 1862), pp. 170-71.

COLOR GUIDE — Serjeant, Col. Henry Jackson's Additional Regiment

Blue	Coat
	Overalls
Buff	Lapels, cuffs, cape
Yellow	Buttons, buckles, sword hilt
White	Waistcoat, epaulette, cockade center, coat lining,
	shirt, musket sling
Black	Stock, hat, shoes, scabbard, garters
Brown	Musket
Silver	Hat binding

Serjeant, Colonel Henry Jackson's Additional Continental Regiment of Foot, 1779 - 1780.

CAPTAIN SILAS TALBOT, CONTINENTAL NAVY, 1779-83

Captain Silas Talbot had the distinction of serving as an officer in both the Continental Army and the Continental Navy. A Rhode Islander, he began his eventful career on land in 1775 as a captain in the 2nd Rhode Island Colony Regiment, and by mid-1777 he was a major in the 1st Rhode Island Regiment of the Continental Line. Wounded at Fort Mifflin on October 23, 1777, Talbot returned to Rhode Island for recovery. There he commanded a number of men-of-war that belonged to the Continental Army, including the sloop *Argo* and the *Hawk*. As an army officer at sea, he is credited with 11 captures and was honored with a lieutenant colonelcy by an act of Congress, November 14, 1778, for his daring capture of the armed schooner *Pigot*. Talbot's talent for sea duty was further recognized when Congress commissioned him a captain in the Continental Navy, September 17, 1779. Regrettably he was captured at sea the next year. Exchanged in 1781, Talbot served in the navy until the end of the war, but never repeated at sea the success he had enjoyed as an army officer.[1]

This illustration is based essentially on a painting of Talbot in naval uniform by Ralph Earl, a leading portraitist of the new republic. The portrait shows extensive gold lace on lapels and coat buttonholes, features not mentioned in early regulations. It also shows the sitter with the medal of the Society of the Cincinnati (a society of Continental Army officers and their descendants) in his left lapel, symbolizing his army service.

Talbot is shown in the blue-and-red uniform that Continental Navy officers wore throughout the war. Although a blue uniform faced with white was recommended in 1777 by a committee of navy officers in Boston, no authorization to adopt it was ever issued by the Marine Committee, and it may never have been worn. No surviving portrait of a Continental Navy officer shows the blue-and-white uniform; the known portraits, such as those of Nicholas Biddle, John Paul Jones, Abraham Whipple, Joshua Barney, James Josiah, and Talbot, all use the blue and red.

The basic uniform of navy officers had been regulated by Congress as early as September 5, 1776. A captain's uniform was blue with red lapels, slash cuffs, stand-up collar, flat yellow buttons, blue breeches, and red waistcoat with narrow lace. Lieutenants and masters were dressed similarly, except that the cuffs were round and faced with red, and the red waistcoat was plain. Midshipmen had red trim around the buttons and buttonholes.[2]

New England, of course, was the birthplace of the Continental Navy and all through the revolution provided its safest havens and most productive recruiting ground.

---

[1] Information on Captain Talbot kindly furnished by the Office of Naval History, U.S. Department of the Navy.

[2] George Henry Preble, "Naval Uniforms," *The United Service*, Vol. II, January-June 1880, p. 744.

COLOR GUIDE — Continental Navy Officer

Blue	Coat, breeches
Red	Lapels, cuffs, waistcoat
Yellow	Buttons, lace, garters
Black	Hat, shoes
White	Cockade, shirt, ruffles, stockings, coat lining

Captain Silas Talbot, Continental Navy, 1779 - 1783.
NEARY
75

COLONEL MICHAEL JACKSON
8th MASS. REGIMENT OF THE CONTINENTAL LINE 1781-1783

Col. Michael Jackson was one of the truly imposing figures of the war for American Independence. By weight, he was the third largest officer in the Continental Army. Exceeding him in girth were only General Henry Knox at 280 lbs. and Col. Swift at 316 lbs. Jackson weighed in at 252 lbs. Jackson, who was a native of Newton, Mass., was a highly regarded officer as well as an imposing figure. He was one of the few regimental commanders in the Continental Line to stay with his regiment throughout the course of the war. As a result he was considered by Washington an especially fine commander and was Washington's guest — a rare privilege indeed — for dinner on many occasions.

The 8th Massachusetts Regiment began its active life in 1777. It was raised in Massachusetts in the months of January and February and made ready to march northward. Small detachments reached Fort Ticonderoga between April and July of 1777. At the evacuation of Ticonderoga in August, the detachment suffered heavily due to lack of clothing and improperly maintained arms.[1] Moving southward the regiment joined General Horatio Gates' army. Henry Michael Jackson's regiment participated in the important Saratoga campaign. Immediately following this campaign, it marched to Valley Forge where it spent the remainder of the year 1777.[2]

The regiment marched out of Valley Forge and joined in the battle of Monmouth. After this service, the 8th was garrisoned in the northern department for the balance of the war.

Col. Jackson is here depicted carrying a favorite possession — an umbrella of green silk. This curious piece of field equipment can still be seen in the Jackson Homestead museum in Newton, Mass. The staff of the umbrella is light brown fruitwood four feet long with a brass tip and ring for hanging the umbrella. Normally it was carried by Col Jackson's waiter (18th century terminology for orderly). A silhouette of Col. Jackson still in the family shows his warlike profile with a large military cockade apparently tinted in red, blue and white. The uniform he is wearing is based on the pattern agreed upon by the officers of the Massachusetts line in January 1781. The color of the coat follows the 1779 regulation and is as follows: blue coat, white lapels, cuffs and cape; white smallclothes (waistcoat and breeches). The uniform in general was to be to the upper part of the kneepan and to be gut high in the neck. The lapel at the top of the breast was to be 3 inches wide and the bottom 2-3/10 inches. The lapel was to be as low as the waist and its wing to button within an inch of the shoulder seam with a small button on the cape. The epaulette is to be worn directly on the top of the shoulder point on the same button with the wing of the lapel. A round and close cuff three inches wide with four closework buttonholes is at the end of the sleeve. The cape was to be made with a peak behind and its width in proportion to the lapels. The pocket flaps were scalloped with four buttonholes, the two inner ones closeworked; the two outer ones openworked and to be set in a curve from the bottom of the lapel to the bottom of the hip. The coat was to be cut full behind, with a fold on each back skirt, and two closeworked buttonholes on each.

Ten openwork buttonholes were on the breast of each lapel with ten large buttons at equal distances. Four large buttons were on each cuff, four on each pocket flap, and four on each fold at the back of the skirts. The buttons on the cuffs and the pocket flaps were to be placed agreeable to the buttonholes. Those on the folds, one on the hip, one at the bottom, and two at the center of the folds at equal distance with those on the lapel. The coat was to button or hook as low as the fourth buttonhole on the breast and as to flaunt at the   bottom with a genteel and military air. Four hooks and eyes on the breast were to go as low as the coat was allowed to button. The skirts were to hook back with a blue heart at each corner and with such other devices as the field officers of each regiment should direct. The bottoms of the coat were to be cut square. The waistcoat was to be single breasted, with twelve buttons and buttonholes on the breast, with pocketflaps, four closework buttonholes and four buttons below the flaps. The breeches were to be made with a half-fall and four buttons on each knee. The small buttons on the waistcoat were to be of the same kind as the large ones on the coat. The number of the regiment was to be in the center of the button with such devices as the field officers should direct. The epaulettes were to be worn agreeable to his Excellency the Commander-in-Chief's orders of June 18th, 1780.

Colonel Michael Jackson, 8th Massachusetts Regiment of the Continental Line, 1781 - 1783.

A fashionable military cocked hat was to be worn, with a silver button loop and a small button with the number of the regiment. A black stock was required when on duty and on the parade.

No edging, vellum lace or indeed any other ornaments not mentioned were to be added to the uniform. No officer was permitted, at any time, to wear any other uniform than that of his regiment.[3]

Given the reputation of Col. Jackson, it is doubtful that he wore any other uniform.

[1] *The Trial of Major General St. Clair*, "Collection of the New York Historical Society, 1880 (New York 1881) p. 101.
[2] *Massachusetts Board of War Records*, Manuscript, Massachusetts Archives, Vol. 153, folio 27.
[3] Elisabeth McClellan, *History of American Costume, 1607-1870* (New York, 1942) pp. 256-257. Note: this order also appears in a number of Massachusetts orderly books for this period.

COLOR GUIDE — Michael Jackson and the 8th Massachusetts Regiment

Blue	Coats
	Top of cockades
White	Lapels, cuffs, capes, coat linings
	Soldier's buttons, straps
	Officer's neck cloth and ruffles at wrists
	Waistcoats
	Breeches
	Center of cockades
Red	Bottom of cockades
Silver	Officer's epaulettes, buttons, hat looping, sword hilt
Green	Umbrella
Brown	Umbrella handle, musket
Black	Hats
	Shoes
	Boots
	Half gaiters, soldier's stock, cartridge box
Crimson	Sash

PRIVATE SOLDIER, THIRD CONNECTICUT LINE REGIMENT, 1778

With the Continental Army's supply system in a state of near breakdown in the winter of 1777-78, General Washington reluctantly allowed the Connecticut authorities to handle their own logistics. The State Council for Safety instructed Governor Jonathan Trumbull in January 1778 to take all necessary steps to deliver clothing to the regular Connecticut regiments. Uniforms for some 4,000 men were to be gathered from local supplies or purchased as necessary.[1] Major John Bigelow of Hartford was appointed Agent Clothier to the Connecticut Line. As a result of Bigelow's work, the state's troops were able to survive the winter at Valley Forge and made a respectable showing at the battle of Monmouth, New Jersey, in August 1778.

The private here wears a light brown coat with red lapels and yellow buttons, green waistcoat and breeches, white shirt, grey stockings, and a black stock around his neck. His belts are white. His hat and cockade are all black except for a brass button holding the cockade looping. (Records show that in 1777 the regiment had worn light brown vests and breeches.)[2] The cartridge box is black and is of the old 19-cartridge capacity which regimental inspection returns show were carried as late as July 6, 1779.[3]

[1] Jonathan Trumbull to O. Andrews, Lebanon, Conn., December 10, 1777, Papers of the Continental Congress, Item 78, Vol. 8, folio 173, Microcopy 247, Roll 91, U.S. National Archives and Record Service.
[2] Clothing Accounts of the 3rd Connecticut Regiment, Samuel Richards, Regimental Clothier and paymaster, Revolutionary Journals and Orderly Books, Box IV, Connecticut Historical Society.
[3] Return of the 3d Connecticut Regiment of Foot in the service of the United States . . . as reviewed by the Inspector General, July 6, 1779, Jacket 43-3, Connecticut Rolls, Revolutionary War Rolls, U.S. National Archives.

COLOR GUIDE — Pte 3d Connecticut Regiment 1778

Light brown	Coat
Red	Lapels
Green	Waistcoat, breeches
Grey	Stockings
Yellow	Buttons
White	Shirt, cartridge box belt, musket sling, bayonet belt
Brown	Musket
Black	Hat, cockade, shoes

Private Soldier, 3rd Connecticut Line Regiment, 1778.

SERJEANT, 10th MASSACHUSETTS REGIMENT, CONTINENTAL LINE, 1782

On the 29th of August 1780, a British merchant fleet, a fleet of 54 sail, arrived at the port of Cadiz, having been taken prisoner by the combined Spanish and French fleets. Taken on board this fleet were elements of two full infantry regiments, 160 cannon and extensive supplies of British military clothing.[1] As part of Spain's contribution to the American war effort, the cargo of soldiers' clothing was sold at a discount to Richard Harrison, of Virginia, the Continental Consul at Cadiz. Between April and June of 1781, Harrison consigned 123 bales, 56 casks and one trunk of clothing to the Clothier General at Boston. Clothing of every description from privates' to officers' coats, waistcoats, breeches, silver-laced officers' hats, light infantry coatees, shoes, and in short every type of clothing was included in the shipments.[2]

When the clothes reached Boston they were for some reason kept in store until April 1782, when they were issued to the New Hampshire, New York, New Jersey lines, the 10th Massachusetts Regiment and the Invalid Regiment. The coats had been during this period dyed to a uniform brown with appropriate facing colors attached.[3] Although these uniforms were of excellent quality, considerable dissatisfaction was expressed by the troops about receiving clothing whose color did not harmonize with the regulation blue. In spite of the dissatisfaction, the clothing was issued. A deserter from the 10th Massachusetts Regiment, one George Durant, "about 35 years of age, 5 feet 7 inches high, light complexion, short sandy hair curled in the neck, light blue eyes, wore away dark brown coat, British worsted laced facings, and old white waistcoat, and white breeches and stockings, a round hat with worsted binding, supposed to be a deserter from the Continental Army — on Wednesday the 22nd inst. hired a chestnut colored mare, . . . Boston, May 26, 1782." Signed Joshua Davis. This announcement was printed in the *Boston Gazette* of 27 May 1782. According to the definitive source for the rosters of the Massachusetts troops, entitled *Massachusetts Soldiers and Sailors in the War of the Revolution*, Boston, 1899, Vol. 5 p. 80, a George Durant enlisted in Colonel Benjamin Tupper's 10th Massachusetts Regiment on April 30, 1781 for twelve months. He was entered as a deserter on 5 May 1782. Our figure is based on this description. According to Colonel Walter Stewart, Inspector of the Northern Army, in June, the regiment had in use 362 coats, 395 vests, 377 woolen overalls, 408 linen overalls, 310 hats, 68 caps, 537 shirts, 194 stocks, 413 pair of hose, 323 shoes, 231 blankets, 1 marquee tent, 13 horsemen's tents and 77 common tents, 49 camp kettles, 1 pick, 420 knapsacks and 431 canteens. Moreover, he wrote, "This Regit. made a good appearance — their clothing is taken very good care of — their arms are in excellent order — but many cartridge boxes indifferent."[4] The serjeant here is seen with buff breeches, a common issue to the Massachusetts troops during the year 1782. He wears on each shoulder a white worsted epaulette denoting his rank and carries a black shoulder belt with a grenadier-type sword. His hat has silver lace, which is a further indication of his rank. The coat is far richer and of better quality than that afforded to other troops.

[1] *Maryland Journal and Baltimore Advertiser*, December 5, 1780.
[2] Richard Harrison to George Washington, Cadiz, March 12, 1781, Manuscript George Washington Papers, Vol. 168, folio 20, Manuscript Division, Library of Congress.
[3] David Brooks to George Washington, Newburgh, April 1st, 1782, Manuscript George Washington Papers, Vol. 194, folio 9, Library of Congress.
[4] Inspection return of the 10th Massachusetts Regiment commanded by Colonel Benjamin Tupper for the month of June 1782, Jacket 20-1, item 10, reel 39, Revolutionary War Rolls, Record Group no. 93, microcopy 246, National Archives and Record Service Collections.

COLOR GUIDE — 10th Massachusetts Regiment 1782

Color	Item	Color	Item
Blue	Officer's coat, bottom of plume	Brown	Serjeant's coat
	Heart on serjeant's turnbacks		Canteen
White	Serjeant's lapels, cuffs, cape, buttons, button hole lace, breeches, coat turnbacks, cartridge box belt, hat band around crown, epaulettes		
	Officer's lapels, cuffs, cape, lining, shoulder belt, trowsers	Grey	Stripes on officer's trousers
	Middle part of officer's plume		Haversack
Black	Hats; serjeant's feather, cartridge box, sword scabbard		Serjeant's stockings
	Serjeant's half gaiters	Yellow	Serjeant's sword hilt
	Shoes	Red	Top of officer's plume
Silver	Binding on serjeant's hat, officer's epaulette, buttons, buckles		

Sergeant, 10th Massachusetts Regiment, 1782.

MAJOR,
SECOND NEW HAMPSHIRE CONTINENTAL LINE REGIMENT,
1781-83

Writing from Fort Ticonderoga in June 1777, Joseph Cilley, Nathan Hale, and Alexander Scammel, colonels of the 1st, 2nd, and 3rd New Hampshire Continental Line regiments, appealed to the New Hampshire Committee of Safety to clothe their troops. The colonels asserted that "our troops have been worse than any in the service."[1] But by mid-1778 the three New Hampshire outfits were uniformed as follows: 1st regiment: green regimental coats faced red with yellow buttons, red waistcoat, green breeches, cocked hats, white shirts.[2] Second regiment: sky-blue coats faced red, red waistcoats, blue overalls, black hats.[3] Third regiment: blue coats lined white, white buttons.[4]

Uniformity of color was attained in November, 1778, when all three regiments received a full issue of clothing imported from France: brown coats with red lapels, collars and cuffs, the cuffs of slashed style, white buttons and lining, lead colored stockings, white waistcoats and breeches, and brown overalls.[5] Hats were not a part of this shipment. For his own uniform of the same style, Colonel Cilley applied to the New Hampshire Board of War for 2 yards of brown cloth, 1½ yards of white cloth, ¼ yard of red cloth, 4½ yards of white challoon, 3½ dozen double washed buttons (white) for coats and 3½ dozen white jacket buttons, twist and silk to trim the same, ¾ of a yard of buckram, a hat, and one pair of silver epaulettes.[6]

The New Hampshire Line's uniform of blue and white was prescribed in the regulations of 1779; however, it appears that in 1782 the enlisted men were entirely clothed in captured British uniforms dyed brown.[7] But some officers continued to have blue uniforms, as suggested by an issue of cloth sold to Captain Enoch Chase of the 2nd Regiment by the state War Office in Portsmouth, N.H., April 5, 1781. He received 2¼ yards cream-colored broadcloth, 2 yards blue cloth, 3 yards of white shalloon, 4 skeins of sewing silk, 4 dozen coat buttons, 3 dozen jacket buttons, 2 hanks of twist, 5 yards of linen for linings, 17½ yards of holland, a beaver hat, a quarter yard white broadcloth, two pair of worsted hose, 6 yards white bath beaver coating.[7]

The uniform laid out for the 2nd New Hampshire Regiment was completely described in an orderly book of the regiment, preserved by the New Hampshire Historical Society. So complete is this regimental order that it merits quotation in full. It has never heretofore been published. Our illustration is largely a reconstruction of this regimental order.

Garrison Orders, March 26th, 1781, New Hampshire Village.

Coat—to extend to the middle of the knee joint middling waist, agreeable to the present fashion.

Facings—2½ inches at the top, 2¼ inches in the middle, 2-1/8 inches at the bottom.

Frog on upper part of the facings—the lower part 2½ inches, the middle 1¾ inches, upper end 2 inches. The frog will be held by the buttons that are set on the shoulders for the epaulette and set up there. The collar the fore part 2½ inches; on the top of the shoulder, 2 inches; the extreme of the collar behind, 3½ inches.

The buttons of the coat to be set on in pairs 2 inches between each button and ¾ inches between the pairs. One pair to be set on below the facings on each side in a line with the vest with false buttonholes to admit of which, facings must be shorter than usual. Round cuffs 2½ inches deep, 4 large buttons on each in pairs, 2 small buttons on the under side of the cuffs or slit.

Two buttons on the upper part of the backfold of the coat to be set against the false buttonholes. The upper one to be set on high as the upper part of the pocket flap, one button on the middle and one on the lower end of each fold.

The Coat to be edged with white—end to have white lining—small blue diamonds on the corners of the folds with narrow Lace and Persion binding around the edges under which will be fixed the hooks and eyes.

One line of narrow lace or Persion binding on the outside of the facings and Collar and round the upper end of the Cuffs—the false buttonholes below the facings and all the buttonholes of the pocketflaps and folds to be laced.

Major, 2nd New Hampshire Continental Line Regiment, 1781 - 1783.

The pocket flaps of the Jacket to be made agreeable to those of the Coat, the buttonholes on the Jacket to be faced and corresponding lace on the opposet breast.[8]

There is also a brief sketch of the pattern of the pocket, indicating that the pocket was four inches on each side, nine inches wide, and was completely outlined in a lace 3/10 inch wide.

The fifer in our illustration is Samuel Odiorne, who acknowledged receipt of five yards of white velvet, 2¾ yards of homespun cloth and one pair of hose due to him as a fifer in the 2nd battalion September 27, 1781.[9]

Boot legs, black ribbon, fabric for shirts, and 2 swords were also provided for the officers.[10]

[1] New Hampshire Colonels to the New Hampshire Committee of Safety, Ticonderoga, June 7, 1777, Papers of the Continental Congress, Item 78, Vol. XI, folio 169-72, Record Group 160, National Archives.

[2] *Freeman's Journal*, August 9, 1778; New Hampshire Archives, Vol. VIII.

[3] Ebenezer Stevens Papers, New–York Historical Society, Vol. XI, Folio 35. Charles M. Lefferts, *Uniforms of the American, British, French and German Armies in the War of the American Revolution*, plate XIV, is a color illustration of this uniform.

[4] Benjamin Stone to John Penhallow, April 15, 1777, New Hampshire Archives, Revolutionary War Documents Series, Miscellaneous, Vol. 5, folio 98.

[5] Public clothing store, Springfield, November 16th, 1778, Return of clothing forwarded to His Excellency, Genl. Washington at Fredericksberg, from the 12th Oct. to the 14th Nov. 1778, War Dept. Collection of Revolutionary War Records No. 27600, Record Group 93, National Archives.

[6] New Hampshire Archives, box 1776.

[7] David Brooks to George Washington, Newburgh, 1 April 1782, George Washington Papers, Vol. 194, folio 9, Manuscript Division, Library of Congress.

[8] Receipt book of James Blanchard in account, New Hampshire 1781-1782, Manuscript Division, Library of Congress. Orderly book of Captain Cherly, 2nd New Hampshire Regiment, Vol. 973.3N532, New Hampshire Historical Society.

[9] New Hampshire Archives, 1901 series, Vol. 35, folio 187.

[10] New Hampshire Archives, 1901 series, Vol. 36, folio 17.

COLOR GUIDE — 2nd New Hampshire

Blue	Officer's coat, diamond on inside of lining
	Fifer's lapels, cuffs, shoulder wings
	Fife case cord
White	Officer's lapels, cuffs, cape, coat lining
	Fifer's coat, waistcoat and breeches and turnbacks
	Fifer's buttons,
	Fifer's half gaiters
	Officer's shirt, neck cloth, ruffles, small cockade
	Piping on fifer's coat
Silver	Piping on officer's cuffs, lapels, cape, pocket, diamond, waistcoat, coat and on button holes on waistcoat, coat pocket, and below lapels
	Officer's epaulette, buttons, cockade looping and button
	Officer's sword and hilt,
Cream	Officer's coat and breeches
Black	Hats, plumes, shoes
	Officer's scabbard, boot legs, hair ribbon
Brown	Fife, officer's boot tops, pulls
Crimson	Sash

Rhode Island State Brigade, 1777 - 1779.

RHODE ISLAND STATE BRIGADE, 1777-79

Colonel, 2nd Rhode Island State Regiment; Drummer, Rhode Island State Artillery Regiment.

A Rhode Island State Brigade, consisting of two infantry batallions of 600 men each and an artillery regiment of 300 men, was raised for 18 months' service by an act of the General Assembly dated December 19, 1776. Each battalion was to consist of eight companies; the artillery regiment, four companies. Along with a bounty of £6, each recruit for the brigade was to receive from the state a blanket, knapsack, musket, bayonet, cartouch box, and canteen. Clothing and other necessities were to be supplied by the state through a quartermaster appointed to each regiment.[1] When the enlistments of the brigade were extended another fifteen months by the General Assembly on December 19, 1777, the bounty was increased to £20 and each recruit was to receive a hat, one uniform coat, two waistcoats, two pair of breeches, three shirts, three pair of stockings, two pair of shoes, one hunting shirt and a pair of overalls.[2]

Due to the presence, after December 1776, of British troops in Newport, and the continued threat of further invasion, the brigade served only within its home state and adjacent waters. Perhaps the most outstanding accomplishment of the brigade was the July 10, 1777, raid led by William Barton, Lieutenant Colonel, 2nd Rhode Island State Regiment, to capture British Major General William Prescott. In whaling boats they slipped across Narrangansett Bay to enter enemy-held Newport. Prescott was caught in bed and brought to rebel lines still in his nightshirt and cap. The British general was eventually exchanged for Charles Lee, Washington's captured second-in-command. This figure of a colonel is based on a contemporary portrait of Barton.

Initially, the brigade seems to have been recruited largely from seamen. Descriptions of deserters during 1777 reveal that blue sailors' jackets lined white, checked flannel shirts, and round hats were the common dress of the 1st State Regiment, while the 2nd mostly wore brown coats, striped trowsers or overalls, and round hats. The artillery regiment had a variety of clothing. No major effort to uniform the brigade was undertaken before 1778.

Papers of Colonel Elliott's artillery regiment in the Rhode Island Historical Society indicate substantial issues to enlisted men during 1778. In June 1779, the officers submitted a list of their wants for the ensuing campaign, including blue broadcloth for 27 coats, buff cloth for the same number of waistcoats and breeches and scarlet cloth for coat facings. In addition they asked for 54 pair of worsted hose, 54 pair of thread ditto, 27 Barcelona, 81 linen handkerchiefs, and linen and cambrick sufficient for 83 shirts.[3]

The musician's uniform is found in a description of Eldridge Spink, Jr., a 12-year-old drummer, 4 feet 8¼ inches tall, light blue eyes and light brown hair, who had on (when he deserted) a blue coat, the seams trimmed with blue and white saddle trimmings.[4] We have added a cap similar to the type worn in 1776 by the Rhode Island Train of Artillery (see Bellerophon's *Caps and Helmets of the American Revolution*).

According to a deserter description of December 13, 1777, in the *Providence Gazette*, the 1st State Regiment had blue-faced yellow uniforms. By the end of 1778, the regiment had received 372 cartouch boxes, 366 belts, 278 coats, 258 breeches, 732 pair stockings, 703 body shirts, 791 pair of shoes, 477 blankets, and 153 hats.[5] Although none of the deserter descriptions for the 2nd State Regiment indicates a uniform, we are assuming that the blue and buff regimentals Colonel Barton is wearing in his portrait are those of the 2nd Regiment. We do know from state records that in 1778, the regiment received from the Council of War at least 74 coats, 100 waistcoats, 99 pair of breeches, 88 hats, 168 shirts, 200 pair shoes, 180 pair stockings, 91 frocks, 92 pair overalls, 96 blankets, 70 knapsacks and 75 stocks.[6]

[1] John R. Barlett, ed., *Records of the State of Rhode Island* (Providence, 1863), Vol. VIII, p. 62.
[2] *ibid.*, pp. 345-46.
[3] Revolutionary War Clothing Accounts, Military Papers Vol. 17, folio 142 (copy no. 141), Rhode Island Archives.
[4] *Providence Gazette*, May 31, 1777.
[5] Rhode Island Archives, *op. cit.*, folio 62, "Account of Clothing delivered for Colo Crary's Regiment."
[6] *ibid.*, "Acct Cloathing Drew from States Store & Del'd by John Reynolds Agt Cloathier for the use of Col Wm Bartons Regt."

COLOR GUIDE — Rhode Island Brigade

Blue	Coats	
	Alternate squares on drummer's lace	
Buff	Colonel's lapels, cuff, cape, waistcoat, breeches	
Crimson	Colonel's sash	
Black	Colonel's hat, drummer's cap; scabbard; shoes	
Brown	Drum body	
Gold	Colonel's epaulettes, buttons, sword hilt	
Red	Drummer's cape, drum loops	

Drummer, Rhode Island Artillery.

DRUMMER, THIRD CONNECTICUT REGIMENT, 1782-83 (Cover)

Commanded by Colonel Samuel Blatchley Webb, the 3rd Connecticut Regiment was constituted of seasoned veterans from Webb's earlier command, known variously as an Additional Continental Battalion or the 9th Connecticut Regiment. As the 9th Connecticut, the unit was outfitted in brilliant red uniforms (see Bellerophon's *Paper Soldiers of the American Revolution*). The uniform shown here is the last type worn by Connecticut troops during the revolution. It was adopted by agreement of the three regimental commanders of the Connecticut line in 1782 and is a modification of the basic uniform prescribed by Congress in 1779. General Washington had urged that the basic uniform of the eastern troops, blue faced with white, be modified to distinguish each state's troops from the others, and also that regimental commanders work out a means of distinguishing the regiments within a given line from each other. The modifications arrived at by Connecticut officers during 1779-81 have not come to light, but the regulation of 1782 was recorded.

CORNET, SECOND REGIMENT OF LIGHT DRAGOONS 1780 (Back Cover)

In recognition of his services as commander of Connecticut Volunteer Horse during the New York Campaign of 1776, Major Elisha Sheldon of Sharon, Connecticut, was appointed by the Continental Congress on 16 December 1776 as Lieutenant Colonel Commandant of the 2nd Regiment of Continental Light Dragoons. The horses of this regiment were to be mares ("No Stallions") white or gray. Each troop was to consist of a captain, one lieutenant, one cornet, one quartermaster, two sergeants, two corporals, one trumpeter, one farrier, and thirty four troopers.[1] To help him raise the regiment, the state of Connecticut arranged for Colonel Sheldon to receive $10,000.00 in January 1777.[2] For its part in assisting the regiment, the Massachusetts Bay Board of War, allowed Sheldon to take whatever horse equipment the Massachusetts public stores could provide.[3] By spring of 1777, Major Benjamin Tallamadge of the regiment could report a full troop at Middlebrook, New York mounted on dapple grey horses equipped with bear skin holsters and black straps. This troop appears to have served General Horatio Gates as vedettes and couriers during the Saratoga campaign. Due to the wooded nature of the country around Albany, no serious horse engagements occurred.

The regiment's first battle was at Pound Ridge, New York in July 1779 when 90 of Sheldon's men and 120 militia were attacked by Banastre Tarleton heading 270 British dragoons, hussars, cavalry and infantry. A running fight occurred, with the Americans losing their British pursuers but also sacrificing their regimental colors and regimental papers.[4] At the time of this engagement, the regiment was the first continental light dragoon unit to have a company of light infantry attached, thus forming the nucleus of a new tactical unit — the legion. It was not until April 1780 that a full issue of uniform clothing was obtained for the regiment. Major Tallamadge succeeded in obtaining 386 suits of clothing consisting of dark green coatees faced with white, white linings, and green cloaks with white capes.[5] The brass helmets had been ordered in January 1778.[6] Our cornet of light horse shown in this full color illustration has a single silver epaulette on the left shoulder and a silver strap on the right to indicate his rank. He also carries a bandolier with a clasp to hold the keeper of guidon pole. The guidon, a troop color, is patterned after an original specimen in the Museum of History and Technology, Smithsonian Institution. (This flag can also be colored in the Bellerophon Book, *Flags of the American Revolution*.) Portraits of Tallamadge and other officers by American artist Jonathan Trumbull show the distinct form of the helmet and other details of the uniform.

[1] *Writings of George Washington* (Washington, D.C., 1932) Vol. V: pp. 386-388.
[2] Jonathan Trumbull Papers, Box 69 Force Transcripts, Library of Congress.
[3] Massachusetts Archives Volume 270.
[4] William F. Imrie "Pound Ridge," *Adjutant's Call* 1963-1964: 12; Pennsylvania Archives, 1st series, Vol VII, (Philadelphia 1853): p. 577.
[5] Elisha Sheldon to George Washington, May 26, 1780, manuscript collection of George Washington Papers, Vol. 136, item 67, Manuscript Division, Library of Congress.
[6] Damaged Account Book, Record Group 59, National Archives.